EXPLORE THE UNITED STATES

# KENTUCKY

Julie Murray

**Big Buddy Books**

An Imprint of Abdo Publishing
abdobooks.com

# abdobooks.com

Published by Abdo Publishing, a division of ABDO, PO Box 398166, Minneapolis, Minnesota 55439. Copyright © 2020 by Abdo Consulting Group, Inc. International copyrights reserved in all countries. No part of this book may be reproduced in any form without written permission from the publisher. Big Buddy Books™ is a trademark and logo of Abdo Publishing.

Printed in the United States of America, North Mankato, Minnesota
102019
012020

THIS BOOK CONTAINS
RECYCLED MATERIALS

Design: Aruna Rangarajan, Mighty Media, Inc.
Production: Mighty Media, Inc.
Editor: Liz Salzmann

Cover Photograph: Shutterstock Images
Interior Photographs: alexeys/iStockphoto, p. 25; AP Images, p. 27 (top); bauhaus1000/iStockphoto, p. 13; Brent Moore/Flickr, p. 28 (top); Chris Humphrey/AP Images, p. 29 (top left); Darron Cummings/AP Images, p. 19; JimMone/AP Images, p. 27 (bottom); Russell Hons/AP Images, p. 29 (top right); Shellphoto/iStockphoto, p. 17; Shutterstock Images, pp. 4, 5, 6, 7, 9 (all), 10, 15, 16, 21, 22, 24, 26 (all), 28 (middle, bottom), 29 (middle, bottom), 30 (top right, middle, bottom); Sven Simon/AP Images, p. 23; vicm/iStockphoto, p. 30 (top left); volgariver/iStockphoto, p. 11

Populations figures from census.gov

Library of Congress Control Number: 2019943176

**Publisher's Cataloging-in-Publication Data**

Names: Murray, Julie, author.
Title: Kentucky / by Julie Murray
Description: Minneapolis, Minnesota : Abdo Publishing, 2020 | Series: Explore the United States | Includes online resources and index.
Identifiers: ISBN 9781532191206 (lib. bdg.) | ISBN 9781532177934 (ebook)
Subjects: LCSH: U.S. states--Juvenile literature. | Southeastern States--Juvenile literature. | Physical geography--United States--Juvenile literature. | Kentucky--History--Juvenile literature.
Classification: DDC 976.9--dc23

# CONTENTS

# ONE NATION

The United States is a diverse country. It has farmland, cities, coasts, and mountains. Its people come from many different backgrounds. And, its history covers more than 200 years.

Today the country includes 50 states. Kentucky is one of these states. Let's learn more about Kentucky and its story!

## DID YOU KNOW?

Kentucky became a state on June 1, 1792. It was the fifteenth state to join the nation.

Cumberland Gap is a famous mountain pass in southeastern Kentucky.

# KENTUCKY UP CLOSE

The United States has four main regions. Kentucky is in the South.

Kentucky shares its borders with seven other states. Tennessee is south. Missouri is west. Illinois, Indiana, and Ohio are north. West Virginia and Virginia are east.

Kentucky's total area is 40,408 square miles (104,656 sq km). About 4.4 million people live in the state.

Puerto Rico became a US commonwealth in 1952.

**DID YOU KNOW?**
Washington, DC, is the US capital city. Puerto Rico is a US commonwealth. This means it is governed by its own people.

★ Regions of ★
the United States

West
Midwest
South
Northeast

CANADA

WASHINGTON
OREGON
MONTANA
NORTH DAKOTA
SOUTH DAKOTA
IDAHO
WYOMING
CALIFORNIA
NEVADA
UTAH
COLORADO
NEBRASKA
IOWA
KANSAS
ARIZONA
NEW MEXICO
OKLAHOMA
TEXAS

MINNESOTA
WISCONSIN
MICHIGAN
ILLINOIS
INDIANA
OHIO
MISSOURI
KENTUCKY
TENNESSEE
ARKANSAS
ALABAMA
GEORGIA
MISSISSIPPI
LOUISIANA
FLORIDA
NORTH CAROLINA
SOUTH CAROLINA
VIRGINIA
WEST VIRGINIA
WASHINGTON, DC
MARYLAND
DELAWARE
NEW JERSEY
CONNECTICUT
RHODE ISLAND
MASSACHUSETTS
NEW YORK
PENNSYLVANIA
VERMONT
NEW HAMPSHIRE
MAINE

PACIFIC OCEAN

ATLANTIC OCEAN

MEXICO

Gulf of Mexico

ALASKA

HAWAII

PUERTO RICO

N
W ◆ E
S

# CHAPTER 3

# IMPORTANT CITIES

Frankfort is the capital of Kentucky. It is located on the Kentucky River. About 27,700 people live there. That makes it one of the smallest US capitals.

Louisville (LOO-ih-vihl) is Kentucky's largest city. Its population is 620,118. Many goods are shipped from its airport and river port. The city is also known for hosting the Kentucky Derby.

LOUISVILLE

LOUISVILLE **is across the Ohio River from the state of Indiana.**

FRANKFORT

FRANKFORT **The current Kentucky State Capitol was built in the early 1900s. It is the state's fourth capitol building since 1792.**

BOWLING GREEN

BOWLING GREEN **is home to Western Kentucky University.**

LEXINGTON

LEXINGTON **Jif peanut butter is made in Lexington.**

Lexington is Kentucky's second-largest city. It is home to 323,780 people. It is known for its beauty. The area has rich soil and fields of bluegrass. Also, the University of Kentucky is located there.

The state's third-largest city is Bowling Green. Its population is 68,401. It is home to important businesses. Chevrolet Corvette cars are one of many products made there!

**DID YOU KNOW?**

Yum! Brands is based in Louisville. The company runs KFC, Pizza Hut, and Taco Bell restaurants.

Many horses are raised on farms near Lexington. This city is known as the "Horse Capital of the World."

# CHAPTER 4

# KENTUCKY IN HISTORY

Kentucky's history includes Native Americans, explorers, and settlers. Native Americans hunted and farmed in present-day Kentucky for thousands of years.

In 1776, Kentucky became part of the Virginia Colony. As settlers arrived in the 1770s, Native Americans fought for their land. Many people died during this time. Still, settlers worked hard to build towns. Kentucky became the fifteenth state in 1792.

Daniel Boone was a famous pioneer. He visited Kentucky for the first time in 1767. Later, he began a settlement there called Boonesborough.

# CHAPTER 5

# ACROSS THE LAND

Kentucky has grasslands, mountains, and forests. It is famous for its wide fields of bluegrass. And, the Appalachian Mountains run through the southeastern part of the state.

Many types of animals make their homes in Kentucky. These include woodchucks, bats, and wild turkeys. Rivers and lakes are home to many types of fish.

**DID YOU KNOW?**

In July, the average high temperature in Kentucky is 88°F (31°C). In January, it is 43°F (6°C).

Cumberland Falls is one of Kentucky's natural wonders. People often visit Cumberland Falls State Resort Park.

# CHAPTER 6

# EARNING A LIVING

Kentucky is a manufacturing and service state. Businesses there make cars, food, and appliances. Many people work for the state and local governments. Others work at the state's major military bases.

Kentucky's land provides the United States with important products. Mines provide coal. Farms produce a variety of crops.

Computer company Lexmark is one of the biggest companies in Lexington.

**DID YOU KNOW?**

Louisville and Lexington form the "Golden Triangle" with nearby Cincinnati, Ohio. This area is where most of Kentucky's people and businesses are found.

The coal from Kentucky's mines helps provide electricity for the United States.

# CHAPTER 7

# SPORTS PAGE

Many people think of horses when they think of Kentucky. This state raises many racehorses. And, it has been home to a famous horse race called the Kentucky Derby since 1875.

The Kentucky Derby is one of three important races called the Triple Crown. The derby is held every May at Churchill Downs in Louisville. Thousands of people attend. Before the big race there are fireworks, parties, concerts, and a parade.

Around 150,000 people attend the derby each year. Millions more around the world watch it on television!

# CHAPTER 8

# HOMETOWN HEROES

Many famous people are from Kentucky. Country singer Loretta Lynn was born in Butcher Hollow in 1932. She often wrote songs about her life. Her first song came out in 1960.

In 1976, Lynn wrote a book called *Coal Miner's Daughter*. It tells the story of her life. Lynn grew up poor in Kentucky. But, she followed her dreams and became the "Queen of Country."

In 2013, President Barack Obama awarded Lynn the Presidential Medal of Freedom.

Famous boxer Muhammad Ali was born in Louisville in 1942. In 1960, Ali won a gold medal at the Summer Olympics. He went on to become the heavyweight boxing champion three different times!

Ali is also known for standing up for his beliefs. He refused to fight in the Vietnam War even though that was against the law.

**DID YOU KNOW?**

Actor Jennifer Lawrence was born in Indian Hills. She is known for starring in the *Hunger Games* movies. She has also acted in several *X-Men* movies.

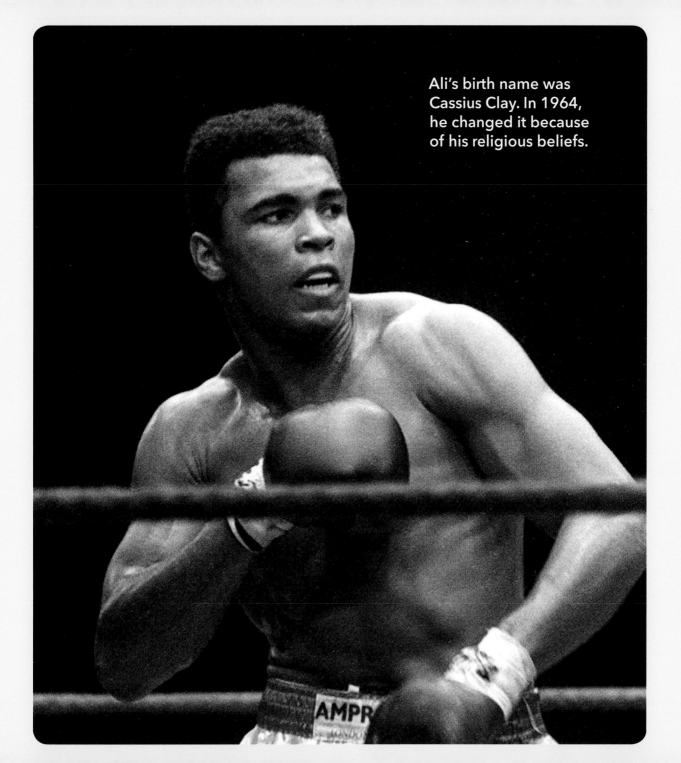

Ali's birth name was Cassius Clay. In 1964, he changed it because of his religious beliefs.

# CHAPTER 9

# A GREAT STATE

The story of Kentucky is important to the United States. The people and places that make up this state offer something special to the country. Together with all the states, Kentucky helps make the United States great.

Daniel Boone National Forest is in eastern Kentucky.

Kentucky's white-fenced
horse farms are world famous.

# TIMELINE

**1792**

Kentucky became the fifteenth state on June 1.

**1875**

The first Kentucky Derby was held at Churchill Downs in Louisville.

1700s

1800s

1900s

Virginia doctor Thomas Walker led a group of explorers to Kentucky. They were the first colonists to see the Cumberland Gap.

**1750**

The **American Civil War** began. Some people from Kentucky fought for the South. But more fought for the North.

**1861**

A special building was completed at **Fort** Knox to store US gold.

**1936**

**1952**

Restaurant owner Harland Sanders (*right*) founded Kentucky Fried Chicken. Over time, it grew into a popular chain of fast-food restaurants.

**2010**

The story of racehorse Secretariat became a popular Disney movie. This real-life horse famously won the Triple Crown in 1973.

**2018**

The University of Louisville women's basketball team won their conference championship!

2000s

Martha Layne Collins became the first female governor of Kentucky.

**1983**

A tornado outbreak occurred on March 2 and 3. Seventy tornadoes hit Kentucky and neighboring states. In Kentucky, 22 people were killed.

**2012**

27

# TOUR BOOK

Do you want to go to Kentucky? If you visit the state, here are some places to go and things to do!

**TASTE**

Eat fried chicken at the Harland Sanders Café and Museum in Corbin. This is where Kentucky Fried Chicken began. You can also see some items from the restaurant's beginnings.

**SEE**

Visit Kentucky Horse Park near Lexington. You can watch horses eat and run in grassy fields.

Kentucky Horse Park hosts many horse shows and competitions.

### CHEER

Catch an exciting college basketball game! The University of Louisville Cardinals and the University of Kentucky Wildcats have popular men's and women's teams.

The University of Kentucky men's basketball team has won the national championship eight times!

### EXPLORE

Tour Mammoth Cave. This is the longest cave system in the world! You can also hike, camp, or canoe in Mammoth Cave National Park.

### REMEMBER

Visit Abraham Lincoln's birthplace near Hodgenville. There's a one-room log cabin like the one his family lived in.

# FAST FACTS

▸ STATE FLOWER
Goldenrod

▸ STATE TREE
Tulip Tree

▸ STATE BIRD
Northern Cardinal

▸ STATE FLAG:

▸ NICKNAME:
Bluegrass State

▸ DATE OF STATEHOOD:
June 1, 1792

▸ POPULATION (RANK):
4,468,402
(26th most-populated state)

▸ TOTAL AREA (RANK):
40,408 square miles
(37th largest state)

▸ STATE CAPITAL:
Frankfort

▸ POSTAL ABBREVIATION:
KY

▸ MOTTO:
"United We Stand, Divided We Fall"

# GLOSSARY

**American Civil War**—the war between the Northern and Southern states from 1861 to 1865.

**appliance**—a machine for the home, such as a refrigerator, that is powered by electricity.

**capital**—a city where government leaders meet.

**diverse**—made up of things that are different from each other.

**fort**—a building with strong walls to guard against enemies.

**grassland**—a large area of grass, with little or no trees.

**region**—a large part of a country that is different from other parts.

**Vietnam War**—a war that took place between South Vietnam and North Vietnam from 1954 to 1975. The United States was involved in this war for many years.

# ONLINE RESOURCES

**Booklinks**
**NONFICTION NETWORK**
FREE! ONLINE NONFICTION RESOURCES

To learn more about Kentucky, please visit **abdobooklinks.com** or scan this QR code. These links are routinely monitored and updated to provide the most current information available.

# INDEX